D0856835

Advance Praise for *Ongoingness*

"After I had my son I looked everywhere for a book that might serve as some kind of mirror. I bought so many silly books. Now I see what the problem was: I wanted a book about time—about mortality. I can't think of a writer who is at once so experimentally daring and so rigorously uncompromising as Sarah Manguso. *Ongoingness* is an incredibly elegant, wise book, and I loved it."

—Miranda July

"The memoir form is shaken up and reinvented in this brilliant meditation on time and record-keeping. *Ongoingness* is a short book but there's nothing small about it. Sarah Manguso covers vast territory with immense subtlety and enviable wit."

—Jenny Offill

"Sarah Manguso's personal meditation on time and memory begins at the center of a dilemma: how to let time go by without losing the life it contains. *Ongoingness* is a diary turned inside out, an answer to the writer's question, 'what do I do with all the words of my life.' It's a quiet argument for letting go and going on."

—Lewis Hyde

"It seemed scarcely possible that, after *The Two Kinds of Decay* and *The Guardians*, Sarah Manguso's work could get more urgent, but somehow it has. *Ongoingness* confronts the deepest processes and myths of life and death: birth, marriage, illness, mourning, motherhood, art. Underwriting this book, as is true of all of Manguso's books, is writing itself. Or, rather, the writing is about itself in the best, most vital sense. Our author/narrator/speaker/heroine is never not asking the most fundamental question, namely, Why live? The seriousness of the inquiry gives this book extraordinary purpose, momentum, and value. I am in awe."   —David Shields

Ongoingness

Also by Sarah Manguso

Ongoingness

the end of a diary

Sarah Manguso

Graywolf Press

The quoted lines on page 7 are excerpted from "When You Are Old" by William Butler Yeats.

This publication is made possible, in part, by the voters of Minnesota through a Minnesota State Arts Board Operating Support grant, thanks to a legislative appropriation from the arts and cultural heritage fund, and through a grant from the Wells Fargo Foundation Minnesota. Significant support has also been provided by Target, the McKnight Foundation, Amazon.com, and other generous contributions from foundations, corporations, and individuals. To these organizations and individuals we offer our heartfelt thanks.

Published by Graywolf Press
250 Third Avenue North, Suite 600
Minneapolis, Minnesota 55401

www.graywolfpress.org

Published in the United States of America

ISBN 978-1-55597-703-0

2 4 6 8 9 7 5 3 1
First Graywolf Printing, 2015

Library of Congress Control Number: 2014950981

Cover design: Kyle G. Hunter

For Adam

Ongoingness

I started keeping a diary twenty-five years ago. It's eight hundred thousand words long.

I didn't want to lose anything. That was my main problem. I couldn't face the end of a day without a record of everything that had ever happened.

I wrote about myself so I wouldn't become paralyzed by rumination—so I could stop thinking about what had happened and be done with it.

More than that, I wrote so I could say I was truly paying attention. Experience in itself wasn't enough. The diary was my defense against waking up at the end of my life and realizing I'd missed it.

Imagining life without the diary, even one week without it, spurred a panic that I might as well be dead. ❖

The trouble was that I failed to record so much.

I'd write about a few moments, but the surrounding time—there was so much of it! So much apparent *nothing* I ignored, that I treated as empty time between the memorable moments.

Despite my continuous effort—in public, in private, in the middle of the night, and in moving vehicles—I knew I couldn't replicate my whole life in language. I knew that most of it would follow my body into oblivion.

From the beginning, I knew the diary wasn't working, but I couldn't stop writing. I couldn't think of any other way to avoid getting lost in time. ❖

I tried to record each moment, but time isn't made of moments; it contains moments. There is more to it than moments.

So I tried to pay close attention to what seemed like empty time. I made my writing students sit silently for twenty, thirty, forty minutes. Then we all wrote about the almost nothing that had happened. I was always running between the classroom and the photocopier so we could read, right away, about the almost nothing that had just happened.

I wanted to comprehend my own position in time so I could use my evolving self as completely and as usefully as possible. I didn't want to go lurching around, half-awake, unaware of the work I owed the world, work I didn't want to live without doing. ❖

To write a diary is to make a series of choices about what to omit, what to forget.

A memorable sandwich, an unmemorable flight of stairs. A memorable bit of conversation surrounded by chatter that no one records. ❖

Why do people keep diaries? Prisoners, explorers, regents—of course. But there are so many others, nobly addressing the entire future.

I was one of the others, but I wasn't writing to anyone.

Inside the cover of one notebook I copied some lines of poetry as a love letter to my future self:

> *When you are old and grey and full of sleep,*
> *And nodding by the fire, take down this book,*
> *And slowly read, and dream of the soft look*
> *Your eyes had once, and of their shadows deep . . .* ❖

Hypergraphia, the overwhelming urge to write. *Graphomania*, the obsessive impulse to write. Look up the famous cases if you're interested. Nothing about them ever helped me with my problem. ❖

Like many girls I was given a diary. The book bore pictures of teddy bears on every page. I wrote in it every now and then out of a sense of duty.

When I was nine I brought the diary to the beach where I went with my parents every summer. My mother reminded me to write in it each night. I didn't enjoy the task and remember her dictating lines like *In the old town center, the shops keep their doors open for all to see.*

I didn't need a diary then. I wasn't yet aware of how much I was forgetting. ❖

I meet people who consider diary keeping as virtuous as daily exercise or prayer or charity. *I've tried for years,* they say. *I start a diary every January.* Or *I don't have the discipline.* They imagine I have willpower or strength of character. *It would be harder for me not to write it,* I try to explain. It doesn't feel like (in one friend's words) *a big fat piece of homework.* I write the diary instead of taking exercise, performing remunerative work, or volunteering my time to the unlucky. It's a vice. ❖

I started keeping the diary in earnest when I started finding myself in moments that were too full.

At an art opening in the late eighties, I held a plastic cup of wine and stood in front of a painting next to a friend I loved. It was all too much.

I stayed partly contained in the moment until that night, when I wrote down everything that had happened and everything I remembered thinking while it had happened and everything I thought while recording what I remembered had happened.

It wasn't the first time I'd had to do that, but as I wrote about the art opening I realized my self-documentation would have to become a daily (more than daily?) practice.

Today was very full, but the problem isn't today. It's tomorrow. I'd be able to recover from today if it weren't for tomorrow. There should be extra days, buffer days, between the real days.

If I allowed myself to drift through nondocumented time for more than a day, I feared, I'd be swept up, no longer able to remember the purpose of continuing.

Twenty-five years later the practice is an essential component of my daily hygiene. I'd sooner go unbathed. ❖

The first volume, a yellow spiral-bound notebook, was disguised as my math notebook, the word *Trigonometry* printed in black on the cover, and on every notebook thereafter, I wrote the name of my current math course. During my first semester of college, I created a digital document called *Differential Equations*. During my second semester, not enrolled in linear algebra as planned (I got a C+ in differential equations), I opened a new file, *Differential Equations 1993*. Every year since then I've opened a new one, hiding everything I thought was important in a file named after a branch of higher math, where, as only a C+ student would, I thought no one would ever look for it.

I still write in little notebooks in diners and on trains, and, after a vigorous editing on the page, I transcribe the remains into *Differential Equations 2014*. ❖

One afternoon I declined a ride from one city to another with a friend who didn't survive his twenties. I didn't think I'd survive the afternoon without spending four hours on the bus back to college thinking and writing about what had happened during my trip. My memory was too full. It was an emergency. I had to empty the reservoir right away.

Nothing had happened, but I still needed four hours to get it into the notebook. ❖

I revised my diary during the day, days later, and some-times years later, with absolute certainty I never wanted anyone to read it.

Everyone I've told finds the idea of my revisions perverse, but if I didn't get things down right, the diary would have been a piece of waste instead of an authentic record of my life. I wrote it to stand for me utterly. ❖

What if I narrate the same memories aloud each night in the same words? What if the memories degrade a bit more each night anyway? What if the recitation becomes rote but functionally useless?

Because I can't reliably answer that question, for twenty years, every day, I wrote down what happened. After I finish writing this sentence I'll do it again.

I'll open the document, scroll down to the end, think to myself that I should write a macro to open the document at the end (which is never the end) instead of the beginning, then look at the keyboard. Then I'll type the date in numerals and points. Underneath, I'll type something in words. Then I'll close the file. I'll reopen it at least once on most days. ❖

I often prefer writers' diaries to their work written intentionally for publication. It's as if I want the information without the obstacles of style or form. But of course all writing possesses style and form, and in good writing they aren't obstacles.

Another friend said, *I want to write sentences that seem as if no one wrote them.* The goal being the creation of a pure delivery system, without the distraction of a style. The goal being a form no one notices, the creation of what seems like pure feeling, not of what seems like a vehicle for a feeling. Language as pure experience, pure memory. I too wanted to achieve that impossible effect. ❖

The first time anyone else read the diary was 1992. On the day I moved into my freshman college dormitory, I reached into the big box of sweaters and diaries and found . . . sweaters.

We didn't think you'd be needing those, said my father. My two new roommates and their parents were there. I didn't say anything. At that time, my diary was mostly about hating my mother. ❖

Two years later, I lent my laptop to my boyfriend, who needed to write five papers in one night, and in the morning, he returned the computer with a little *Word* icon right in the middle of my otherwise empty desktop. *Please Read Me, Sarah*, he'd called it. The document began: *I just read your diary. All 75 pages of it* . . . I don't remember how it went other than that he not only failed to apologize but represented the act as a gesture of compassion, since I so clearly needed his expert help in evolving into a better person.

He'd just learned, among other things, that I could barely feel him inside me. ❖

After college, I lived in an apartment with four room-mates, one of whom I sometimes curled up and slept with. One morning I saw he'd opened the document along with all the letters I'd ever written him; his name was in the file names. After an initial denial he admitted he'd opened the files but, in a fit of remorse, closed them before reading them.

I could have protected the document with a password or padlocked or hidden the computer, but I didn't care enough to inconvenience myself. The diary wasn't a trove of secrets; it was, simply, everything. I might as well have hidden myself from view. I still don't care whether anyone reads it. ❖

Shortly after the turn of the millennium, I read the diary from beginning to end. Finding nothing of consequence in 1996, I threw the year away.

I'd already shredded the volumes I wrote in high school—not to keep them from others but to keep them from myself. So it seems I didn't want to remember everything.

I wanted to remember what I could bear to remember and convince myself it was all there was. ❖

A few years after I threw 1996 away, another friend asked if he could try to hypnotize me.

He wanted to know why I was still thinking about someone I'd gone to bed with just once, months earlier, and barely seen again.

So did I. I lay down.

My friend swung a pendant from a string above my face, then asked me to close my eyes.

Why won't you give up this imaginary problem?

The answer, suddenly accessible to me for the first time, surprised me: *Because I don't want to.*

I wrote it in the diary. ❖

I don't remember the chronology of those I embraced past the first five. I'd have to consult the diary.

I kept seeking and finding the exquisite moment. By the eighth, I'd already be seeking the ninth and tenth.

Around the thirteenth, it finally got to me. Finally, even I had to notice I'd become intolerant of waiting. My forward momentum barely stopped for the length of the touch.

I thought my momentum led to the next person, but in fact it only led away from the last person.

My behavior was an attempt to stop time before it swept me up. It was an attempt to stay safe, free to detach before life and time became too intertwined for me to write down, as a detached observer, what had happened.

Once I understood what I was doing, with each commitment I wakened slightly more from my dream of pure potential. ❖

It was a failure of my imagination that made me keep leaving people. All I could see in the world were beginnings and endings: moments to survive, record, and, once recorded, safely forget.

I knew I was getting somewhere when I began losing interest in the beginnings and the ends of things.

Short tragic love stories that had once interested me no longer did.

What interested me was the kind of love to which the person dedicates herself for so long, she no longer remembers quite how it began. ❖

When I first saw the portrait of a sixteenth-century court page, I fell instantly into a deep and enduring love.

The page was in love with a girl that the duke had chosen for one of his cousins. When the duke learned of the page's courtship, he forbade them to meet again, but after three years he gave in and offered them twenty-four hours to marry. They were married immediately and had eight children.

The wonderful thing about genetics, another friend said, *is that you* can *in fact sort of be with him.* She's right—if you ever meet my husband you might notice a resemblance. ❖

During the first few years of my marriage I was highly susceptible to the previous day. I was convinced the marriage would soon be over, but it wasn't over. The problem was my inability to experience it as ongoing.

Another friend wrote, *Marriage isn't like having a boyfriend or girlfriend but a little more so any more than gold is helium but a little more so. The inner shell of electrons fills and then the next one goes into the next shell, changing everything.*

Marriage isn't a fixed experience. It's a continuous one. It changes form but is still always there, a rivulet under a frozen stream. Now, when I feel a break in the continuity of *till death do us part*, I think to myself, *Get back in the river.* ❖

In my diary I recorded what had changed since the previous day, but sometimes I wondered: What if I recorded only what hadn't changed? *Weather still fair. Cat still sweet. Cook oats in same pot. Continue reading same book. Make bed in same way, put on same blue jeans, water garden in same order* . . . Would that be a better, truer record? ❖

Living in a dream of the future is considered a character flaw. Living in the past, bathed in nostalgia, is also considered a character flaw. Living in the present moment is hailed as spiritually admirable, but truly ignoring the lessons of history or failing to plan for tomorrow are considered character flaws.

I still needed to record the present moment before I could enter the next one, but I wanted to know how to inhabit time in a way that wasn't a character flaw.

Remember the lessons of the past. Imagine the possibilities of the future. And attend to the present, the only part of time that doesn't require the use of memory. ❖

Sensory memory lasts about two hundred to five hundred milliseconds after perception. Then it starts to degrade.

Working memory, or short-term memory, allows recall for a period of several seconds to a minute.

Long-term memory can store larger quantities of information for a longer duration, potentially until the end of life. It may be divided into procedural memory, used in learning motor skills, and declarative memory, used in conscious recall.

Declarative memory may be further subdivided into what scientists call semantic memory, which concerns facts taken independent of context, and episodic memory, which concerns personal experiences that occurred at a particular time and place.

Autobiographical memory is generally viewed as equivalent to episodic memory.

I record these facts dutifully, as if they dignify this writing with something more real than my memories—as if they reveal. ❖

The least contaminated memory might exist in the brain of a patient with amnesia—in the brain of someone who cannot contaminate it by remembering it. With each recollection, the memory of it further degrades. The memory and maybe the fact of every kiss start disappearing the moment the two mouths part. ❖

If I considered the act of procreation as essential to the world's general ongoingness, I could almost accept it as an obligation of being alive.

I believed that parturition would honor the force that, in the nineteenth century, joined my earliest ancestors I know by name, and the forces joining anonymous pro-creators for centuries and centuries before that, and so on back to the beginning, to the first sexually differentiated animals.

And then, someday, maybe, someone will have needed me to produce one of their ancestors, and that fact of my parturition, that fact and my name, will be the last any-one remembers of me. All the rest of me will be gone, no longer anyone's burden. ❖

When my grandfather got old, he started emptying the apartment he shared with my demented grandmother. Or maybe these events happened coincidentally.

He didn't throw anything away. He drove it the quarter mile to my parents' place—one day a stack of moisture-warped paperbacks, one day a box of colored pencils, and so on. They kept some of it. His things, at least, would keep going after he ended.

When they got old, my parents started emptying their own apartment. They're selling their things on the internet. I don't know where anything is going.

I knew I was grown up when I spent time with them and felt not just the weight of my old memories but the weight of theirs, from when they were children. ❖

When I'm back with my own memories I drink a glass of wine or a cup of coffee. It helps soften their pressure, but the effect fades. Then I think I should practice grace for what I've been given to remember, but whatever I do, I can't seem to forget what I want to forget.

And then I think I don't need to write anything down ever again. Nothing's gone, not really. Everything that's ever happened has left its little wound. ❖

For most of my life I claimed that my earliest memory took place in a corner of the kitchen. I stood at the counter, knowing I'd be scolded for having taken cookies from the cookie jar. But of course that wasn't the first thing my brain learned and kept.

If I'm to believe the child-care books, the first thing I learned and kept was the identity of my mother. ❖

I remember being three, standing at eye level with the drawer in my mother's night table, the white porcelain knob pierced by a tarnished screw, saying *When am I ever going to be four?*

When I was four I went with a group of children into a nature preserve, where someone pointed out items of interest.

With great excitement he reported the discovery of a lady's slipper, a highly endangered thing.

Each child was led to an opening in the bramble. High branches shaded us.

I was led to the opening. A hand must have pointed to a bloom, but I didn't know to look for a flower. I stood, solemn, seeing nothing, brooding on the phrase *lady's slipper*, wondering what it was. I never saw it. The mystery was enough. It was better. Then I moved aside for the next child. ❖

When I was twelve I realized that photographs were ruining my memory. I'd study the photos from an event and gradually forget everything that had happened between the shutter openings. I couldn't tolerate so much lost memory, and I didn't want to spectate my life through a viewfinder, so I stopped taking photographs. All the snapshots of my life for the next twenty years were shot by someone else. There aren't many, but there are enough. ❖

When I was fourteen, it was cloudy on the night I looked through a telescope at the comet. *I'll see it when I'm eighty-seven,* I thought on the way home, not caring. ❖

When I was twenty-three I began seeing a psychotherapist because I couldn't bear the idea that, after the end of an affair, all our shared memories might be expunged from the mind of the other, that they might no longer exist outside my own belief they'd happened.

I couldn't accept the possibility of being the only one who would remember everything about those moments as carefully as I tried to remember them.

My life, which exists mostly in the memories of the people I've known, is deteriorating at the rate of physio-logical decay. A color, a sensation, the way someone said a single word—soon it will all be gone. In a hundred and fifty years no one alive will ever have known me.

Being forgotten like that, entering that great and ongoing blank, seems more like death than death. ❖

Maybe the best way to remember anything accurately is to write it down and forget it, and then, only at the last moment of your life, to recall it—like listening to a broken tape by hand-feeding it one last time through the tape player.

During the age of the cassette tape, it seemed that everyone was talking about doing that. It was always some high romantic tale, the only live recording of a secret show or the last letter from a long-lost friend.

I never did it. Maybe everyone was lying. No matter. It's still a decent metaphor. ❖

Could I claim a memory even if I couldn't access it via language? Or was I writing as if it never had happened?

I didn't mind that perception is partial or that recollection is worse, but I minded that I didn't know why I remembered what I remembered—or why I thought I remembered what I remembered. ❖

I assumed that maximizing the breadth and depth of my autobiographical memory would be good for me, force me to write and live with greater care, but in the last thing one writer ever published, when he was almost ninety years old, he wrote a terrible warning.

He said he'd liked remembering almost as much as he'd liked living but that in his old age, if he indulged in certain nostalgias, he would get lost in his memories. He'd have to wander them all night until morning.

He responded to my fan letter when he was ninety. When he was ninety-one, he died.

I just wanted to retain the whole memory of my life, to control the itinerary of my visitations, and to forget what I wanted to forget.

Good luck with that, whispered the dead. ❖

The experiences that demanded I yield control to a force greater than my will—diagnoses, deaths, unbreakable vows—weren't the beginnings or the ends of anything. They were the moments when I was forced to admit that beginnings and ends are illusory. That history doesn't begin or end, but it continues.

For just a moment, with great effort, I could imagine my will as a force that would not disappear but redistribute when I died, and that all life contained the same force, and that I needn't worry about my impending death because the great responsibility of my life was to contain the force for a while and then relinquish it.

Then the moment would pass, and I'd return to brooding about my lost memories. ❖

Lives stop, but life keeps going. Flesh begets flesh.

Great cathedrals were built by generations of stonemasons to whom the architect was a man who might once have greeted their grandfathers' grandfathers. How agreeable, then, to believe in God.

To set stones on stones not for the architect but for eternity.

The Latin epitaph in one seventeenth-century cathedral translates: *Reader, if you seek his monument, look around you.*

The words are carved in a disk of black marble set beneath the center of the dome. The disk was placed there by the architect's son.

It's easy to imagine the great man, but try to imagine the son who knows his father's cathedral will be loved longer than the flesh of his flesh. ❖

The oldest known cave paintings are thirty thousand years old. Along with abstract markings and pictures of animals, they include images of human hands.

It seems that the painters pressed their hands against the walls, blew pigment from their mouths onto the walls, and then lifted their hands away.

Then they walked out of the cave, marked with red ochre from fingertip to wrist.

The catalog of emotion that disappears when someone dies, and the degree to which we rely on a few people to record something of what life was to them, is almost too much to bear. ❖

Another friend inherited a collection of ceramic bowls that used to belong to her great-great-great-grandmother. *I like the fact that they break,* she said, *so that I can glue them back together.*

Before my husband went into surgery to have his shattered nose reconstructed, the anesthesiologist told us she'd give him a benzodiazepine intravenously.

It causes anterograde amnesia, so when my husband whispered *I love you* directly into my ear, I whispered back, *You aren't going to remember this.* ❖

When I became pregnant I struck something mortally. Not just myself, symbolically; my son, actually.

The partly made flesh wriggling inside me was already mortal. ❖

During my pregnancy I couldn't remember anything. Information seemed to enter my memory and dissolve.

The diary was of no help.

Emerging from the sickening exhaustion of the first few months, I began to see the work I might do next—this, an assemblage of already exploded bits that cohere anyway, a reminder that what seems a violent interruption seldom is. ❖

Goldfish are said to possess legendarily short memory spans, but in fact they can recall information—such as certain sounds—for up to five months, or so one report claims.

I'm told that even a newborn, in its first months outside its mother's body, remembers the underwater sounds of the womb. ❖

I developed the amnesia that some people call *pregnancy brain.*

Heavily pregnant when I heard my friend's father had died two years earlier, I sent condolences at once, hysterically sorry. My friend wrote back. I'd sent a letter two years earlier. I didn't remember sending it.

Then another friend told me his apartment had been burgled. *How lucky that the dog wasn't hurt!* I wrote back. He'd put the dog down months before. I hadn't remembered that, either.

I scrambled to remember the dead in order—of course an eighteenth-century composer was dead, and all the people who died before I was born. My grandparents all were dead. Recent deaths of those I knew only by their work—a novelist, a monologist. I remembered which of my friends were dead. Another friend's stepmother, in a coma for years, had died earlier that year. *Good,* I thought, *I haven't forgotten them all.* ❖

When I was almost nine months pregnant, my mother-in-law began receiving hospice care.

My doctor wouldn't permit me to cross the ocean to see her. My husband didn't want to miss the birth of our son. And he didn't want to miss the death of his mother, the woman who raised him.

I drank quarts of raspberry-leaf tea, trying to trigger early labor.

Six thousand five hundred miles away from each other, two unplannable moments prepared themselves.

My husband's phone rang. It was his stepsister, calling from his mother's hospital room. *Yes,* he said. A few moments later he said, *Hi, Mom!* I hadn't heard him say it for days. My heart beat hard, as if it knew. ❖

My husband photographs everything: bound hanks of insulated wire on the train platform, clouds at sunset out the jet window, the shape of my foot as I sleep.

When he was fired from his job, he cleared off his hard drives. Then he gave back the company's computers. That night he discovered he'd forgotten to copy the last photographs he'd ever taken of his mother.

In one of the lost photographs, she holds her head in her hand. She turns toward the glass doors that open onto the porch over the canal. She is skeletal, her body no longer able to derive nutrition from food.

She looks uncharacteristically hopeless, as if the picture represented the moment that she, who had outlived her sudden-death prognosis by five years, would not go on. ❖

She was given twenty-four hours to live on the day I was told my cervix was 50 percent effaced.

Three weeks before her only grandchild was born, she joined her old horse, who had fallen suddenly ill only months before and was awaiting her patiently in the earth. ❖

Then I became a mother. I began to inhabit time differently. It had something to do with mortality. I kept writing the diary, but my worry about the lost memories began to subside. ❖

Nursing an infant creates so much lost, empty time. Of the baby's nighttime feeds I remember nothing. Of his daytime feeds I remember almost nothing.

It was a different nothing from the unrecorded nothing of the years before; this new nothing was absent of subjective experience. I was either asleep or almost asleep at all times.

Day and night consisted of the input and output of milk, often in an emergency, but the emergencies all resembled each other. At dawn I noticed a pile of tiny damp blankets and tiny damp clothes on the nursery floor, but I never remembered replacing the green shirt with the yellow one.

In my experience nursing is waiting. The mother becomes the background against which the baby lives, becomes time.

I used to exist against the continuity of time. Then I became the baby's continuity, a background of ongoing time for him to live against. I was the warmth and milk that was always there for him, the agent of comfort that was always there for him.

My body, my life, became the landscape of my son's life. I am no longer merely a thing living in the world; I am a world. ❖

In my twenties I stopped to write every time I happened upon beauty. It was an old-fashioned project. Romances were examined in detail. Each one was new.

My thirties were filled not by romance but by other writing. In the diary I logged the words I wrote and the light or heavy passes I took through existing manuscripts. Virtuous activities such as exercise and housekeeping also were logged. The rhapsodies of the previous decade thinned out.

Toward the end of my thirties and into my forties, entries became further abbreviated. Most of the sentences started with verbs. *I* is omitted from as many sentences as possible, occurring only for emphasis. I logged work and health—symptoms, medications, side effects. Housekeeping was no longer noted. If I read or looked at or heard something extraordinary, I named it, but as one ages, fewer things fall into this category. Reflection disappeared almost completely.

Of a concert by a band I've liked for almost twenty years, listened to most recently about five years ago, but never seen live until this week, I wrote only *Still know every word.* Twenty years ago, the sentence would have been twenty sentences.

Though I try to log only the first time he does yet another extraordinary thing, the diary is now mostly about my son. ❖

Sometimes the baby fed at seven thirty and cried until feeding again at eight thirty.

My life had been replaced with a mute ability to wait for the next minute, the next hour.

I had no thoughts, no self-awareness, just an ability to sit with a little creature who screamed and screamed.

Waiting for the baby to feed or stop feeding or burp or pass wind or yellow liquid shit I postponed showers, phone calls, bowel movements. I ignored correspondence because I had no energy even to say *I am so tired,* and no one cared that I was tired—who isn't tired? Before I had the baby I remember feeling tired all the time. But after he joined me I could spend four days in two rooms, pajama-clad, so tired I was almost blind. ❖

I used to be twenty. Then I was twenty-one, twenty-two, and so on. And then I became a mother and could no longer even distinguish the difference between twenty-one and twenty-two or the difference between thirty-eight and thirty-nine.

I was at once softer and harder. The hardness was a capacity for pain that would otherwise have interrupted the soft, almost bodiless calm in which I held the baby. ❖

Soon after his mother died, my husband's dead father's best friend's ex-wife died. The best friend is the only one left. My husband said the man's name. *That leaves him,* my husband said. *That leaves him, of the people who have known me since I was born. And then my childhood will be truly gone.* ❖

Another friend wrote to ask all the desperate questions I used to ask before I became a mother. *How old were you? How long were you married? How long did it take?*

I wrote back, *One of the great solaces of my life is that I no longer need to wonder whether I'll have children.* ❖

Time kept reminding me that I merely inhabit it, but it began reminding me more gently.

In a dream I found an old-fashioned windup metronome on my desk. A man's voice behind me: *Is that really a metronome on your desk?*

In another dream an old woman told me that at my age, she wished she'd known that *the soul never stops appearing.* ❖

Perhaps it was all the years studying the piano repertoire of the great prodigies, or perhaps it was studying alongside some actual prodigies—one of them was blind—but when I turned seventeen I became convinced I had fallen into a life of irreversible failure.

The stench of failure—I felt it coming to cover me.

Now I am old enough to know what I'll never accomplish. I will never be a soldier, a physicist, a thousand other things. It feels like relief.

Sometimes I feel a twinge, a memory of youthful promise, and wonder how I got here, of all the places I could have got to.

I use my landlady's piano as a writing desk. ❖

My students still don't know what they will never be. Their hope is so bright I can almost see it.

I used to value the truth of whether this student or that one would achieve the desired thing. I don't value that truth anymore as much as I value their untested hope. I don't care that one in two hundred of them will ever become what they feel they must become. I care only that I am able to witness their faith in what's coming next.

I no longer believe in anything other than the middle, but my students still believe in beginnings. Ask them, and they will tell you that everything is about to start in just a moment, just one more moment.

That beginner's hope, the hope that ends with the first failure—when I was with the baby I felt that hope all the time. ❖

Trapped in a party conversation with two young people, I wanted to wait with them in the smoky hallway for fifteen years so I could hear what they'd say when they were forty. ❖

In another dream my tiny toothless son had all his teeth. I'd looked away long enough for all the teeth to emerge, even the back molars, the teeth beating time in months, in years, his full jaws a pink-and-white timepiece.

In the next dream his downy hair had grown very long and I needed to cut it off with dull scissors. Again his body had recorded time passing, time that had escaped my notice. ❖

For months the baby woke at seven, fed, fell asleep at eight thirty, woke at ten, fed, fell asleep at eleven thirty, and so on for the rest of the day. I'd made him into a milk clock.

Every hour was part of a ritualized ceremony of adding or subtracting milk. A river of milk flowed in and out and around him. He floated down the milk river toward the rest of his life. ❖

One explanation for the loss of preverbal memories maintains that after acquiring language, one forgets how to access those preverbal memories.

As I watched the baby play with his toys I remembered an orange plastic panel fixed to the rails of my own crib. A round red rubber air bladder the size of my fingertip. A bell. A black-and-white crank that clicked. A blue-and-red sphere that spun fast in its housing and looked purple.

My brain had stored this memory—all the textures and colors and shapes and sounds. If you had asked me six months earlier if it were possible to retain infant memories into adulthood I would have said no, but I carried this memory without looking at it for thirty-eight years. ❖

As I fed the baby with a little spoon I remembered a spoon scraping dribbled food from my chin and tipping it back into my mouth. That dribbled food, already tasted and diluted with saliva, never tasted good.

What else was on the orange panel? The bell and the crank and the spinning ball rang and cranked and spun. The air bladder forced the clapper up. I could see it moving up and striking the silver bell anchored by its silver bolt.

I remembered wanting to press the little red bladder again, again, again. Spinning the ball again, again, again. Wanting to see the purple. Wanting to hear the bell. I liked that it kept ringing.

Then I remembered a mirror.

I believed I was trying to remind myself of how it had felt to be wordless, completely of the physical world—that even before my body was an instrument for language it had been an instrument for memory. ❖

It used to be that things always reminded me of a lot of other things.

Then, for eighteen months or so, they didn't. In the diary I recorded only facts. Minutes of nursing, ounces of milk, hours of sleep.

Things were just themselves. I was too exhausted or hormone-drunk or depressed to think of anything that resembled anything else.

That's how things appear to an infant. ❖

One postpartum day it took me forever to remember the word *obsolete*. Another day, *suggestible*. Another, *fennel*. Does the mother of an infant need a smaller lexicon? Does she need a specifically limited lexicon? Did I not need to think about fennel then? About abstractions? ❖

I remember from childhood that, from the point of view of a child, a mother is a fixed entity, a monolith, not a changing, evolving human organism who is qualitatively similar, in many ways, to a young person.

Recently I became not quantifiably old but qualitatively old. Old as a state of being. As an acceptance that I've more or less become the person I had a chance to become.

I've been basically the same person since I had my son. I know this isn't true for all new mothers, especially those who are younger than I am (and most of them are). But I feel like a monolith now. I've emerged from a gauntlet, and it has something to do with having become a mother, and it has something to do with having become qualitatively old, and it has something to do with having run out of time and life to perceive and ruminate and record my minutes and days in the diary.

What I'm saying is that I have become, in a way, inured to the passage of time. I'm not really paying attention to what's happening to me anymore—no longer observing steadfastly the things that have changed since yesterday. ❖

I'm watching my little son change, though, from day to day and minute to minute. Watching him learn things is like watching a machine become intelligent, or an animal become a different animal. It's terrifying and beautiful, and this has all been said before.

On the island where my husband grew up and where his mother lived and died, we see a rainbow every day. Not just a segment of a rainbow fading in and out but the whole bright bow of it, sometimes in double and triple arcs. Rainbows are so common there, they print them on the drivers' licenses. They are no less amazing for their prevalence. Ditto birds, trees, stars, clouds, children, and so on. To the laws of supply and demand the real world is immune. ❖

When the baby was eight months old, I realized I'd stopped identifying with the man saying *Hi, Mom!* and felt myself becoming the mother who hears him say it, the mother who will someday leave her boy alone. ❖

The essential problem of ongoingness is that one must contemplate time as that very time, that very subject of one's contemplation, disappears.

My prose began to judge or summarize its subject before it took any time to observe that subject. I couldn't help attaching that tendency to the subject itself: the wild velocity of motherhood, an enforced momentum forbidding contemplation.

The tendency to summarize rather than to observe and describe—would taking that time to observe and describe be selfish, wasteful, nonmaternal time?

Is it possible to truly observe one's own child, as a writer must, while also simultaneously loving him? Does a mother have something like writer's block—*perceiver's block?* ❖

Left alone in time, memories harden into summaries. The originals become almost irretrievable.

One day the baby gently sat his little blue dog in his booster seat and offered it a piece of pancake. The memory should already be fading, but when I bring it up I almost choke on it—an incapacitating sweetness.

The memory throbs. Left alone in time, it is growing stronger.

The baby had never seen anyone feed a toy a pancake. He invented it. Think of the love necessary to invent that. In a handful of years he'll never do it again. An unbearable sweetness.

The feeling strengthens the more I remember it. It isn't wearing smooth. It's getting bigger, an outgrowth of new love. ❖

Since the baby was born I still occasionally wonder whether I should have a baby, whether I should get married, whether I should move to this or that city I've already moved to, already left. All the large questions still float about me, and in its sleep-deprived dampened awareness of the present moment, my memory treats these past moments as if they're all still happening.

I've never understood so clearly that linear time is a summary of actual time, of All Time, of the forever that has always been happening. ❖

A year postpartum, my memory was still afflicted. I enjoyed writing because within days, I forgot what I'd written, and rereading it was like reading a letter from someone else.

In class my students repeated what they claimed I'd said during the previous class, and, not remembering the words as my own, I found myself approving of them vaguely. ❖

My life felt full before I became a mother, but I've found that trying to say that I prefer having the baby to not having him sounds aggressive. In fact I'd felt affronted, before I was a parent, when parents told me, even in the gentlest terms, that they preferred having their children to not having them.

Maybe the trouble is that the shape of life is elastic, that it can feel and be full at variable levels of fullness. Or maybe we're poor judges of our own lives' fullness. Or maybe the concepts of emptiness and fullness are poor metaphors for happiness, if in fact happiness is what we're talking about. ❖

Let me put it another way: when I am with my son I feel the bracing speed of the one-way journey that guides human experience. ❖

The trouble was that I failed to record so much, I wrote, but how could I have believed that if I tried hard enough, I could remember everything? ❖

I wrote about an illness once I was seven years into a re-
mission that lasted four more.

I didn't know it yet, but the illness, which still isn't over,
wasn't the real problem. Thinking about it was the problem, and I don't think about it anymore. Not in the obsessive, all-consuming way I used to.

I used to harbor a continuous worry that I'd forget what
had happened, that I'd fail to notice what was happening. I
worried that something terrible would happen because
I'd forgotten what had already happened.

Perhaps all anxiety might derive from a fixation on
moments—an inability to accept life as ongoing. ❖

Once I'd spent two years hobbled by an impaired memory, I worried less about everything I was forgetting.

I forgot to buy milk this week. I forgot to file taxes last year. And on I go. ❖

The best thing about time passing is the privilege of running out of it, of watching the wave of mortality break over me and everyone I know. No more time, no more potential. The privilege of ruling things out. Finishing. Knowing I'm finished. And knowing time will go on without me.

Look at me, dancing my little dance for a few moments against the background of eternity. ❖

Why, then, should I continue writing the diary?

In it I digest the time that passes, file it away so I no longer need to think about it, *and if I spent all my time thinking about the past I'd stop moving into the future,* I begin to write, but no—I'd keep moving. How ridiculous to believe myself powerful enough to stop time just by thinking.

There's no reason to continue writing other than that I started writing at some point—and that, at some other point, I'll stop. ❖

Often I believe I'm working toward a result, but always, once I reach the result, I realize all the pleasure was in planning and executing the path to that result.

It comforts me that endings are thus formally unappeal-ing to me—that more than beginning or ending, I enjoy continuing. ❖

Before the baby was born, the diary allowed me to continue existing. It literally constituted me. If I didn't write it, I wasn't anything, but then the baby became a little boy who needed me more than I needed to write the diary. He needed me more than I needed to write about him.

The time I spent sitting and nursing and holding the baby and cleaning up his messes could have borne the worry from me as completely as I bore the baby, which in my experience marked a change of mind that by now seems permanent. ❖

Before I was a mother, I thought I was asking, *How, then, can I survive forgetting so much?*

Then I came to understand that the forgotten moments are the price of continued participation in life, a force indifferent to time. ❖

Now I consider the diary a compilation of moments I'll forget, their record finished in language as well as I could finish it—which is to say imperfectly.

Someday I might read about some of the moments I've forgotten, moments I've allowed myself to forget, that my brain was designed to forget, that I'll be glad to have forgotten and be glad to rediscover as writing. The experience is no longer experience. It is writing. I am still writing.

And I'm forgetting everything. My goal now is to forget it all so that I'm clean for death. Just the vaguest memory of love, of participation in the great unity. ❖

When I remember how this document began, I remember it as something I used to worry about. ❖

My son goes happily on.

One of his first words was *bamboo*. Everywhere we went, he called out to the bamboo that was or wasn't there. *Bamboo!* He called his bear *Bamboo* and fell asleep whispering its name.

Time passed. He grew accustomed to the world. He learned more words.

His bright hair grew long.

Everything is new. His first lizard. His first funeral. Now we measure his age in years.

The future happens. It keeps happening.

The man is still alive, but the boy is gone. The light is out.

His light is out yet it shines triumphant from the next of the living, and when their time is up, their potential spent, the light will move along to the next brightest, and the next.

A flash—and I'm gone, but look, the churn of bodies through the world of light unending.

Look, here we are, even now—

Afterword

I asked a few friends whether they thought I should excerpt the diary in this essay, praying they would say no.

None of them did.

But I didn't want to read the thing, so I tried to reason my
way out of the task. I envisioned a book without a single
quote, a book about pure states of being. It sounded almost religious when I put it that way. I wasn't sure what I
meant, but I hoped it sounded convincing. A book about
pure experience couldn't quote sources. Its only source
could be experience itself.

I was afraid that if I read the diary, I'd have to change
what I'd written about it from memory. And producing
even those few thousand words had been so arduous, I
couldn't bear the thought of having to rewrite them.

But I was even more afraid of facing the artifact of the
person I was in 1992 and 1997 and 2003 and so on. Time
punishes us by taking everything, but it also saves us—
by taking everything. I'm still ashamed of things I said
and did in front of one other person even if that person
is dead.

I reread my favorite books to make sure they're still per-
fect, but rereading them wears away at their perfection.
I imagined how sick I might feel after reading the diary,
the writing that stands in for my entire self.

It was while reading a letter from a childhood friend who continues to provide health care to people in underserved communities that I realized the jig was up. If I was never going to place malaria pills into the hands of the destitute, I needed to get my act together. I had to be sure I wasn't keeping anything from the world that might help it along. If the point was to write things that prevent people from committing suicide, the least I could do would be to read my own diary. Just in case.

I realize how grandiose that sounds, but when your job is to think and write about yourself, the stakes start to appear artificially, comically high. And they must, for without them, I wouldn't write at all. I'd spend the day reading the internet. I'd be about half-done by now.

As luck had it, a few weeks after making the big decision, I boarded a plane for a six-hour trip. I'd prepared for it by bringing nothing to read except my diary. The plane took off. Beverage service began. I drank half a cup of bitter coffee and opened the first of the twenty-three files.

As I read it I copied the passages I thought people might find interesting. There were some potent bits about social class. A few sexual oddments. By the time I got to 1995 I was on my way. What a year that had been.

After I'd skimmed about a hundred thousand words, I looked at what I'd collected, expecting a well-curated assortment of tidbits—something like ten pages of a David Markson novel.

It was not like that.

The collection was hopelessly arbitrary. I realized I'd have to read the diary many more times to ensure I was collecting the best excerpts, and many more times after that, once a form began to flicker in the collection's murk, and I knew I didn't have the time or the stomach for that. Just rereading my adolescent townie disapproval of the first twenty days of college was enough to make me want to tear out the chips or transistors or whatever it is in a computer that makes it remember things.

My troublingly arbitrary collection strategy was no less arbitrary than any arbitrarily systematic plan—for example, collecting the fourteenth day of every month or the first sentence of every thousand. The arbitrariness bothered me, not knowing whether I'd chosen the best bits, if indeed there were any that could be designated as such.

But the even greater problem was that no individual diary entry had been written to make sense by itself. It led neither away from the previous day nor toward the following day. It possessed no form separate from the greater form, which itself was almost formless—which itself was just accumulation, just *day after day after day after day.*

Imagine a biography that includes not just a narrative but also all the events that failed to foreshadow. Most of what the diary includes foreshadows nothing. Most of what it includes happens in the present and disappears. (Did I mention that I write the diary in present tense? I do.)

The threat of writing to an audience becomes only more present a danger as time passes and one's audience increases, I once wrote and believed. And forgot. And read again, and now believe again.

The only thing I ever wrote that wasn't for an audience was the diary.

I could excerpt and revise maybe a year or two as a stand-alone piece of writing, but to include a year or two (which years would I choose?) would only distract from *Ongoingness*, which is about the whole thing, not just a couple of years. Not just the best parts. It's about the diary as a single item, an indivisible behemoth of English prose.

I decided that the only way to represent the diary in this book would be either to include the entire thing untouched—which would have required an additional eight thousand pages—or to include none of it.

I didn't know how to present to an audience a document that had been written for no audience, and I knew I couldn't ask my editor to edit an almost-million-word document possessing no goals regarding coherence or form.

The only way I could include my diary in this book about my diary, then, was to refer to it and then continue on.

Imagine it as dark matter or as one of the sixty-seven confirmed moons of Jupiter or whatever real thing you nonetheless must take on faith.

April 2014
Los Angeles

Acknowledgments

To Jim Behrle, Meghan Cleary, Kayla Gillespie, Sheila Heti, Chelsea Hodson, Jennifer L. Knox, Irene Lusztig, Frank Manguso, Judith Manguso, PJ Mark, Ted Mulkerin, Maggie Nelson, Ethan Nosowsky and everyone at Graywolf, Julie Orringer, Martha Ronk, Mirtha Santizo, David Shields, Zadie Smith, Marya Spence, Lorin Stein, Noelitta Tailiam, Antoine Wilson, Dean Young, the John Simon Guggenheim Foundation, and Adam Chapman, to whom this work is dedicated—my ongoing gratitude.

SARAH MANGUSO is the author, most recently, of *The Guardians: An Elegy for a Friend*, named one of the top ten books of 2012 by *Salon*. Her previous book, the memoir *The Two Kinds of Decay*, was named an Editors' Choice by the *New York Times Book Review* and a Best Book of the Year by the *San Francisco Chronicle* and *Time Out Chicago*. Her essays have appeared in *Harper's*, the *New York Review of Books*, and the *New York Times Magazine*, and her poems have been included in four editions of the Best American Poetry series. She is the recipient of a Guggenheim Fellowship and the Rome Prize. Born and raised near Boston, she now lives in Los Angeles.

Book design by Ann Sudmeier. Composition by Bookmobile Design and Digital Publisher Services, Minneapolis, Minnesota. Manufactured by Edwards Brothers Malloy on acid-free, 100 percent postconsumer wastepaper.